A Note to Parents

DK READERS

Reading Mission

is
or
n

ographs
er

different
s that

are only a general guideline.

No matter which level you
select, you can be sure that you
are helping your child learn to
read, then

LONDON, NEW YORK, MUNICH,
MELBOURNE, and DELHI

Australian Managing Editor Rosie Adams
Series Editor Deborah Lock
Designer Adrian Saunders
Production Shivani Pandey
Photographer Leon Mead

Reading Consultant
Cliff Moon, M.Ed.

Australian Reading Consultant
Fran Burns BEd(Prim)DipRRec

Published in Great Britain by Dorling Kindersley Limited
80, Strand, London, WC2R 0RL

2 4 6 8 10 9 7 5 3 1

A Penguin Company

Published in Australia by Dorling Kindersley Pty Ltd

A CIP record for this book is
available from the British Library

ISBN 1-74033-493-0

Colour reproduction by Colourscan, Singapore
Printed and bound in China by L. Rex Printing Co., Ltd.

The publisher would like to thank the National Library of Australia
for their kind permission to reproduce the image: Earle, Augustus,
1793–1838. 'Desmond, a NSW chief painted for a native dance'.
Call number: PIC T99 NK12/61 LOC Box A35,
National Library of Australia.

All other images © Dorling Kindersley Limited.
For further information see: www.dkimages.com

Models: James Mead, Luke Mead, and Bea Mead

See our complete catalogue at

www.dk.com

DK READERS

BEGINNING TO READ ALONE **2**

Outback Adventure
Australian Holiday

Written by Kate McLeod

A Dorling Kindersley Book

James and his little brother Luke were excited because they were going on holiday with their parents. They lived in Perth, Western Australia and were going to Broome, a remote place in the outback.

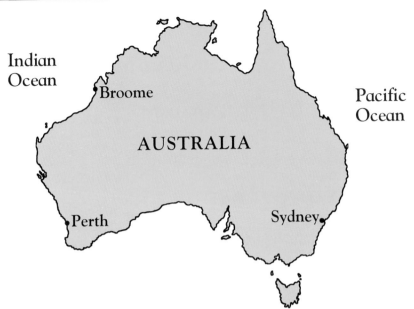

On holiday, they hoped to go fishing and walking in the bush.

James wanted to catch some big fish, and Luke could not wait to go swimming in the sea.

Broome

Broome is a town on the northwest coast of Australia.
It is famous for the pearls found in the ocean nearby.

When the family arrived in Broome,
they went to a campsite
near the beach.
Straight away they all raced
to the water for a swim.
Then Dad hired a boat
to go fishing.
James was lucky –
he caught four fish.

Dad lit a campfire to cook the fish
for dinner.
They were delicious!

At the beach, the boys discovered
giant footprints in the rocks.
"I think it's a dinosaur's footprint,"
said James excitedly.
"I've found one, too!" cried Luke.
"It might be from a Megalosauropus
(Me-ga-luh-SORE-uh-pus),"
said Mum.

The Megalosauropus lived
in northern Australia.
They were carnivores,
which means they ate meat.

Fossils
Dinosaurs lived
between 230 to 65
million years ago.
Their bones and
footprints turned
hard in rocks to
form fossils.

The next day, the whole family
went bush walking.
Luke discovered two giant mounds
of earth.
They were enormous termite nests.

"Wow," said Luke.
"Just imagine how many termites live in these huge nests."
"Thousands," replied James.
"The nests are like termite blocks of flats."

Termites

Termites are small insects that feed on wood and plants. They build giant nests above the ground during the wet season.

The boys climbed over some rocks
and found a cave.

Inside the cave, there were painted
figures on the rocks.

The paintings had been made
with red, yellow and white clay.

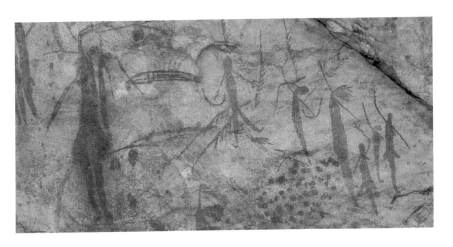

In the paintings, James could see people hunting.

"These were probably painted thousands of years ago by Australian Aborigines," explained Mum.

Aborigines

Aborigines have lived in Australia for thousands of years. They hunted animals and gathered berries and plants for food.

The next day, the family went
to a beautiful beach in Broome.
James and Luke saw horses for hire
and asked if they could have a ride.
After being helped into the saddles,
James and Luke rode their horses
through the water and on the beach.
At the end of their ride, they saw
some other riders.

"Look!" said Luke.

"Those people are riding camels."

"That must be a bumpy ride!"

replied James.

It was raining the next day, so the family visited the pearling museum. They found out about the history of pearl diving around Broome. They saw old costumes that pearl divers used to wear.

James held a large oyster shell.

Metal helmet

Diving suit

Divers used metal helmets to help
them breathe under water.

"They look very heavy," said Luke.

"It must be hard to swim with them
on," James added.

Pearls collected from oyster shells.

James asked his Dad about pearls.
"They are the oldest precious gem,"
said Dad.

"Oysters grow deep under the water
on the ocean floor," said Mum.
"Divers jump off boats and swim
down deep to collect the shells.
When they break open the oyster
shells, they hope to find a pearl inside."

Oysters

When a piece of sand gets into the shell, the oyster coats the sand with layers of skin, which harden to make a pearl.

James and his family went to
a muddy beach to find crabs.
The crabs live in burrows under
the sand and among the rocks.

They come out to find food
on the beach.
When a big crab came out,
James caught it with his hook.
He was careful not to let it pinch
his fingers or toes.

The next day, James and Luke went
to an outback station, or farm.
It was a huge cattle station,
as big as a city.
James met a boy called Pablo,
whose family lived at the station.
James and Pablo went to watch
jackaroos, or cowboys, rounding
up the cattle.

Station
Stations are large
farms in outback
Australia.
Sheep and cattle are
kept on stations, and
horses are used to
round up the cattle.

James and Pablo had lots of fun exploring the station together. At the river, they used the soft bark from the paperbark trees to build boats.

They raced the paperbark boats down the river.

In the afternoon, James and his
family went on a long walk through
the bush around the station.
It was hot, so they found a billabong,
or pool, and jumped in for a swim.

Colourful butterflies
fluttered around the billabong.
"That one looks like a rainbow,"
said Luke.

James, Luke and their parents spent the next day at the Broome Bird Observatory.
The observatory is where scientists catch and count birds, so they can find out how they behave and where they fly to and from.

Hundreds of birds

Over 200 species of birds visit northern Australia every year. They migrate from all over the world.

They watched the scientists catching the birds with netting.

James was even allowed to hold one of the young birds.

On the last day of their holiday,
the family went for a sightseeing
flight in a helicopter.
They flew over massive rocks called
the Bungle Bungles, which the
Aborigines call Purnululu.

"I wish we could stay!" said James. Mum replied, "We'll have to come back soon for more adventures."

Outback facts

Australia is a big country and not many people live outside the main cities. The huge areas where few people live are called the outback. Usually it is hot, dry and dusty, but if it rains, green grasses and leaves appear and the wild flowers bloom.

A station is a large farm in the outback with thousands of cattle and sheep.

In Australia, people who work with the cattle on the stations are called jackaroos. Jackaroos usually ride horses or motorbikes to round up the cattle, but on huge stations they use helicopters.

Billabongs are beautiful pools that are found in the outback. They are often surrounded by gum trees and bushes, and are usually close to rivers.